The Man at the Well

By

Daniel Phillips

All scripture verses are from the
KJV Version of the Bible

This book was printed in the United States of America.
To order additional copies of this book contact:
Lion's Den Ministry
1190 North Mingo Road
Tulsa, OK   74116
Or
www.amazon.com

FWB
Publications
The Best is Less

The Woman At The Well

Meets The Man At The Well

Table of Contents

Acknowledgments

I wish to thank David "R" Kirby. My friendship with him goes back to 1972. He has developed into an outstanding Cognitive-Behavioral Psychotherapist and college professor. He is the one who originated the basic concept for this book. Also, I need to express thanks to my brother, Don, for encouraging me to write this book.

Most of all, I am deeply grateful to my wife, Wanda Phillips. Her valuable suggestions and reading come from her self-giving spirit. All is an expression of her supreme acts of love for me which is truly an expression of grace.

Danny Phillips

A Story of Grace

This is a story about the mystery of grace—the effects of grace and how it relates to redemption. When you pursue after an awareness of grace and redemption you learn about the heart of God.

Grace and redemption always should address the emotional hurts and the overwhelming lack in life. You may wonder if there is a need for another story about the woman at the well. It is by looking thoughtfully at the story that you can realize your own emotional hurts and lack in life. You can see your need for God's grace and redemption.

This story shows the Heavenly Father seeking to redeem fallen man by His grace in the person of Jesus. How it is that someone can catapult into moments where they encounter God? The woman at the well meeting the man at the well is that story.

There are four main characters: the woman at the well, Reuben, Jesus and the centurion Longinus. These characters reveal their thoughts, and each chapter demonstrates where God reveals His grace to them.

Terms

1. *The Second Mile*—In Matthew 5:41 Jesus states, "Go the second mile" concept. Roman law stated that Jewish males could be required to carry mail for at least one mile.

2 *Cursus Publicus*—Those who carried the mail for the republic.

3. *Angaria*—The word used to denote the compulsory service in forwarding imperial messages. Dictionary of Ancient History

4. *Woman at the Well*—She is not named in the Bible; however, some faith traditions give her the name Photine. In this book, she is given the nickname Delight Days by her father.

5. *Man at the Well*—This is the name that Delight Days uses for the Christ. Messiah is Hebrew for the "anointed one". Christ is Greek for "Messiah".

6. *Jacob's Well*—The place where Jesus meets the Samaritan woman in John 4:4-42. It is located outside the city of Sychar. The well is at the southeastern entrance of the valley between Mount Ebal and Mount Gerizim. The well had a fresh, pleasing taste. The New Interpreter's Dictionary of the Bible, Volume 3.

7. *John 4:4*—This verse tells us that Jesus must go through Samaria. There was a great divide between how the Samaritans and Jews viewed each other. Most Jews went around Samaria to get to Galilee from Jerusalem.

8. *Samaritan Pentateuch*—The Samaritan Pentateuch was their own copy of the first five books of Moses. In their Pentateuch there is an addition to Exodus 20:17, affirming Mount Gerizim as the holy site designated by God. Jewish belief sees Jerusalem as the place of God. The New Interpreter's Dictionary of the Bible, Volume 5.

9. *Longinus*—The name given to the centurion at the cross per some religions.

10. *Jehoram and Reuben*—These names are used for the two thieves who hung beside Jesus on the cross. The Bible is silent about their real names.

11. *Elder Josiah*—This character is based on a 96-year-old personal friend, Owen. His wisdom is the inspiration for this character.

The Birth of a Thief

Reuben pauses to listen for sounds as he wonders what happened to the cool night air. With the sound of his heart pounding in his ears, he pauses to listen. "I need water—water to refresh myself," Reuben whispers. The night was moonless and the stars didn't help much with the blackness. Hot and tired, he realizes, as he wipes the sweat from his eyes, that he has been running from the Roman soldiers since the second hour of darkness.

Needing some water to refresh himself, Reuben discerns that he is now slowing down. All he hears is his heart pounding in his ears. Sound travels well in the desert night and after a few more minutes of rest he will be able to hear what the desert has to say.

Reaching into the fold of his robe, he wonders if the purse is still there. As his hand touches the purse, his thoughts return to what has happened. Reuben is a thief and the purse in his robe is not his. It belongs to the Jew who set his camp up a little too far from his fellow travelers. Reuben is a good thief, with quick hands, nimble fingers, and fast and light feet. He can change his appearance and speech to look like a Jew from Judea or the Samaritan that he is.

However, Reuben's skill of disguise would not help him tonight. After he had stolen the purse from under the Jew's pillow, Reuben made his getaway like numerous times before. This time, as he fled, his foot came down on a small twig. Trouble found Reuben the moment the sound of the breaking twig fractured the silence of the camp. Reuben froze, waiting to see if it was enough to awaken the camp. Slowly, turning his head his heart stopped. A young boy was sitting up in his bed, looking at Reuben. In the glow of the dying fire, the boy saw the purse and let out a piercing yell. In an instant, Reuben was running in a direction away from the camp. His only thoughts were getting as far away as he could.

After some time had passed, he realizes it is getting close to mid-morning. He should have been home hours ago. Being careful to stay away from the road has slowed him down. His mind flashes back to last night's simple robbery gone bad.

All he had to do was be quiet and move fast, which he was doing, when he burst through the middle of the camp of Roman soldiers. The soldiers were just taking notice of the sounds of his pursuers when he entered their midst. They were as surprised as he was. Where did they come from? Earlier in the evening, just before dusk, he had scouted out the area around the travelers' camp to see if there was anyone he needed to be aware of. The travelers had quit the chase and the soldiers took up the pursuit. He knew the night had just become longer for him.

Kneeling and looking toward the sky during his long run through the night, Reuben realizes that the celestial clock is telling him he has another couple of hours before reaching home. He hears a sound a short distance away, coming from his left. He is disappointed because he needs to go left. That means it will be nearly mid-day before he can get that cool water from the well of Sychar. He always tries to be home before dawn so he can go unnoticed into his house. Reuben never does any of his stealing near Sychar, always traveling at least a day's journey from there, to keep the town's people from knowing what work he actually does.

Lately the town's elders have been questioning him about his work, suspecting that he might be a thief. He started out being an honest day laborer doing odd jobs. But after several days of searching and not finding any work, and as he was walking home in the night, he came across a caravan. He was able to steal a little food and a flask of oil, which he sold in Nain of Galilee. When he couldn't find honest work, stealing had become his second livelihood and was fast becoming his only livelihood. Soon, he will have to move to another village in Samaria. Standing up, Reuben silently moves toward home.

Mid-Morning

It is mid-morning when Delight Days realizes that the day is getting warmer. The easterly breeze is carrying in the heated air from the desert. Why couldn't the winds be from the west which carries a chance of rain and cooler temperatures? As she prepares to go to Jacob's Well, she thinks about her nickname. Delight Days is not her real name, but the name handed down to her by her father.

As a young girl she was told that she brought her family joy and satisfaction. Her father was a Jewish man that had met her Samaritan mother by Jacob's Well. It is said that it was love at first sight. They loved each other so deeply. She still thinks of her parents' love that brought her into the world. They loved and cared for her as deeply as they loved and cared for each other.

Her thoughts quickly turn to Reuben. He may be coming home today, although it is late. He nearly always shows up just before dawn. If he comes today, he will want fresh water to drink. A moment of bitterness comes to her mind as she reminds herself that she is now a social outcast in the village of Sychar.

It hadn't always been like this. In the early days, before the divorce from her third husband, the village accepted her. Those were the days she could draw water during the cool of the morning with the other village women. But now, things are different. Delight Days has been married five times in her thirty-four years here on earth with no children from any of her marriages.

Her first and second marriages were to two brothers, Amos and Boaz. Amos was a good, Godly man, and her first love. She had just turned fifteen when Amos asked her father if they could marry. He worked

13

hard during that year for their betrothal, building a simple house, with the help of his father. With his inheritance and her dowry, they started their marriage blessed. Amos could really touch her heart with his affections. His tender respect toward her and his love and worship for Adonai moved her. They were partners in every positive sense of the word. Life together meant everything. Both had the typical dreams and aspirations of the young, and such dreams tend to only allow for happiness. They tried for a family, but it didn't happen. This was alright, they thought. It just takes time and it was enough that they had each other for now.

She remembered how Amos would smile at her with his eyes, and a rush of joy, peace, and comfort would wash over her. On nights when the barking dogs of Sychar woke up the whole village, Amos would light a lamp. She can still remember his eyes as the flame danced in them. Whatever the unmet needs of their lives were, those eyes, those sparkling eyes, which smiled at her many times a day, seemed to make life perfect. She shivers as she recalls the day her life of happiness veered off path, when the light left Amos' eyes forever. Who knew crossing paths with the cursus publicus, or mail couriers, would change her life so drastically.

As Delight Days arrives at the well, it is now mid-day. Walking to the well allows her mind to wander back in time – a time of happiness before that fateful day. She thinks back to the time when Amos and his brother Boaz had taken a herd of sheep into Bethany of Judea to sell.

On the way home from selling the sheep, the brothers met a cohort of Roman Soldiers. Amos was forced to carry a mail pouch for the courier who didn't have a horse and was traveling on foot. After the required Roman mile, Amos bent over and placed the mail pouch at the feet of the courier. At the precise moment he was rising up, a centurion turned his horse and gave it a hard kick in the ribs. The horse kicked out with his hind legs and one hoof sent a crushing blow to her sweet husband's head. Instantly knocked unconscious, the sparkling, smiling eyes became cloudy and his smile went blank. In less than an hour, her first love's body lay lifeless in the dirt by the side of the road. That day she learned to hate "angaria" which is the involuntary forced labor from the invaders who conquered this land. The death of Amos brought the tragedy of sadness to her life.

Boaz became her second husband because of the custom whereby if a brother dies before he has an heir, his brother will become the husband to carry on the dead brother's name. Boaz was like his brother in his love for Adonai, yet he didn't love Delight Days and she didn't love him. Boaz died from fever in the early spring of the fourth year of their cold marriage.

Camri was Delight Day's third husband and she knew it was a mistake. He knew she had nearly starved during the winter following Boaz's death. That is when her life started changing in all aspects of living. Carmi was pagan and worshiped Baal instead of Adonai. At first, Carmi was a relief from the past terrible winter. He was not as good as her first two husbands, but he treated her fairly.

Then something changed. It was as though something awakened in him- something like a demon. He became sinister, like a hungry and angry lion. No longer was Delight Days treated with respect, but he began to demean her every chance he could. His anger and physical abuse, in time, would become very intense, even to the point that she feared for her life.

After two years of a shameful marriage, he gave her a Bill of Divorcement. As they sat in the divorce proceedings, in front of the town's elders, with him lying and belittling her, she couldn't say a word in her own defense. Women were not allowed to speak.

She remembered it well. For her the hurt was because of the hateful looks from some of the elders. Elder Josiah, who before had extended help to her in times of need, seemed to have a sadness about him. Here she was, a three time loser in marriage, twice by being a widow and now a divorced woman with no children. That was when she was asked to stop getting water from the town's well in the cool of the morning. With a fourth of a mile to go, Delight Days feels her trip has been uneventful. Hot winds and dusty roads bring thoughts to her mind, causing her to think of her last two husbands. Dathan was her fourth husband, and Enos her fifth husband.

Both of these men knew her life. They were not well off men, but lived comfortably. Life is sometimes hard to survive. They were older, well past their prime. All they wanted was a woman who they could work. She was willing to marry them even knowing life might be hard.

Dathan was not a gentle or kind man. He had no passion for anything or anyone, least of all her. Enos was different. He seemed to really care for her and would often help with the chores. He had a passion for life. Thankfully, I had Enos. In some ways, he reminded me of my first husband.

Reflecting about life, Delight Day's thoughts turn to Reuben- the man Delight Day is in a relationship with now. Reuben treats her well enough, and he always has enough money so they don't go hungry. She wonders if Reuben will be home today.

"Yes," thinks Delight Days, "I am a couple of years older, so would Reuben ever marry me?" That question has been with her since the first year they were together. Now, she wonders if he will leave. It seems that lately Reuben is getting a restless spirit. Was it because he has found someone new, or does he want to leave Sychar?

Lately, as she did her work about town, she would overhear rumors about Reuben being a thief. Every time she would ask him about what he was doing, he just went silent.

This water pot seemed to be heavier today, on her shoulder. Not wanting to waste any water, she always tried to be careful with her pot. As she walks in the hut, Reuben startles her, so some water spills on the floor.

He looks tired, dirty and thirsty, like he has been traveling all night and half a day. Taking a long drink from the water pot, water runs down his chin and onto his dirty clothes. He tells her thanks, as he starts to prepare for his bath. It is good to see him home, even if she must go and get more water for him to clean up. Heading back to the well, her heart is lighter for she will not have to be alone.

Delight Days knows that she will be worn out tonight. Two trips to the well will do that. It was then she realizes that her mind is also tired. The reason is the question that is always on her mind. What is it that Reuben does? He leaves at night and is gone for days. Sometimes he is gone for up to two weeks.

He really looks tired today. He is covered with dust and dirt. The sandal on his right foot looks like the leather strap is about to break. As heat waves dance in the bright mid-day sun, the air seems to be hotter. Reuben has been good to buy food, but where does he get his money? Lately, he has been so jumpy. He becomes very nervous when he hears horses on the road below the hut.

This type of life is not what she had dreamed about. Her dreams had been to live with Amos and they would add on to that little place they had. Over the years, she woke up to the sad reality that dreams are just that- - dreams. They gave hope in her early days, but life now is misery. Broken dreams and broken hope bring fear, confusion and harshness. Reuben did say one day he would build a better house. But for Reuben it is always later, not today.

Halfway to the well, she wonders why she is doing this. She doesn't know. Here, at this point on the road, is where she stops to look in the sky for clouds. When clouds drift past the sun, there is a comforting shade, even for a moment. Not today. This is her life. No comfort from the heat. Because much of life is comfortless, she remembers Deborah. She says that the sameness of day after day brings a dark mood. To her mind, it is unbearable. Delight Days misses Deborah, her childhood friend. Sometimes they can find a place to talk, but because she is considered an outcast, she has to be careful. Is this the way things are for all women? This struggle of life. A destiny of nothing ever changing.

With resolve in her heart, as she walks up to the well, she says to herself, "I survived even in the sameness of life." Looking upon her leather rope and leather bucket, she sees that it is in need of repair. Both are getting old. Sometimes, because of the heat and cold, it is hard to draw the water. It takes more energy to draw the water in the extreme heat. Elder Josiah says, "Life has many paths". It seems her path is always the same--going to the well.

Turning towards home, with the water pot, she wonders if Reuben wants to stay with her. Lately he watches the road more. Does he think someone is watching for him? The other day, Deborah walked by and whispered, "They are saying Reuben is a thief." Oh, Delight Days hopes not. The community will turn away from her even more.

Here is the halfway point. She always takes a long drink. She always tries not to let the water run down her chin. Today, she spills more water than she normally does. For some reason, that she cannot tell, she feels totally rejected by life. At her age, surely one would have some understanding about how to handle life.

Early on Reuben would help her overcome the feeling of gloom. Now, he is consumed by his own needs. She fears he is facing his own dark side. It is almost like he doesn't want to live here anymore. If he leaves, will he tell her, or just go? She really wonders what he does.

I Will Not Forget

"It is close to evening", thought Longinus, the centurion. The details of last night had not escaped him, but this is the first time he can reflect on it-- yesterday was long for his soldiers. He always had these marches to expose the new legionnaires to his command.

As a centurion he had found if he spent a week with the new men, that his command was easier, since new recruits found service sometimes overwhelming. If he can forge these men into a working group, they will find military service not as hard. So, here he was in the middle of the desert with ten new legionnaires and Antonio, his trustworthy soldier. Usually on their first night out they never have a fire. Fire can give away so much in the night.

While he was thinking about the hike tomorrow, Antonio walked up and informed Longinus that there was some type of pursuit heading their way. Listening for the sounds that carry on the night breezes, his men moved close by. It seemed that there was a group of men shouting and heading toward the camp.

Moving a few feet away from his men, he tries to catch meaning from the shouting. Looking intently into the dark, he willed his eyes to see in the darkness. There! Yes, it was a faint sound, but he can't see anything. There it is again! It was the sound of footfalls.

Listening and looking, he stood still. Just then, there was a man in his face. He could make out his form. Quickly he reached out, grabbing at the man. His hand grabbed at the darkness, feeling the brush of the robe.

The stranger stumbled and fell as three men from the caravan who were pursuing him rushed into the camp. Antonio lit a torch. In the light, a face revealed itself. Again, he reached out to grab the stranger but Longinus missed. As he cursed, the lit torch revealed the three men. "Quick", they said as they tried to catch their breath, "Stop him, he's a thief!" For a thief, he was fast on his feet.

"Antonio, take five men and give chase," Longinus commanded. At the same time, he directed two soldiers to build a fire so he could question the three men. Turning toward the fire, he took a moment to commit the face to memory. He whispered to himself, "I will not forget that face." After reflecting about the incident, he slowly drifted off to sleep.

As the dawn begins to chase away the darkness of the night, Longinus sits looking into the fire. Today he will allow his men a whole day of rest. Who was that thief? Longinus knows there has been an increase in robberies this past year. It seems that whoever the thief, or thieves are, they are very good at it.

As the log cracks and breaks into the fire, sparks shoot upward, lighting the breaking dawn with hundreds of tiny, flickering lights. He knows he likes being a centurion; being a centurion, he answers to Pontius Pilate, Governor of Judea. Life has been good for him. Six years ago, he was made a centurion, one who commands one hundred men. Military life is never easy, but being a commander has suited him.

It was a year ago in which all commanders were put on notice. "The robberies have to stop!" declared Pilate. Yes, Samaria is not as bad as Galilee or Judea, but it is becoming worse.

Realizing the air is cooler now, Longinus pulls his cloak tighter as he thinks about the past events. What happened was rare, a thief in the middle of the night, running right into the camp. The swiftest runner gave chase, but not even Antonio, the fastest soldier, could catch the thief.

Looking into the fire, a new idea begins to form. To catch a thief, one has to think like a thief. Suddenly, the wind shifts, blowing the smoke into Longinus' eyes, and forcing him to change position. As he yawns, he begins to ponder about how to catch the thieves.

What to do with this slippery band of thieves? It is in the early morning glow of the fire that a thought begins to grow. Tomorrow, Antonio and Longinus will ride toward Jerusalem. In a week, they will have a meeting with Pilate.

Antonio has no idea what is going to happen. The only way this plan can succeed is to be quiet about it. No more than a dozen people can know this plan. It must be a great deception.

As the fire dies down, the camp takes on a ghost-like feel. The wind is ebbing and flowing. The stars are fading. The smell of the smoke and the quiet of the camp are pushing his eyes to close. The day will begin soon, and he should get some sleep. In a week, he hopes to start his plan with Pilate.

Gone

Reuben has now been home for a week. As Delight Days draws water she wonders why Reuben has stayed inside the hut these last few days. The water pot feels especially heavy today, but thankfully there has been a break in the weather making the air a little bit cooler. Her father called days like today "Blessed Days". Carrying this heavy pot of water brought a sweet memory and smile to her as she thought of him. "Delight Days are what you bring into my life, so your nickname is "Delight Days", her father would tell her.

Never having any brothers or sisters allowed her parents to dote on her. She misses them greatly. They helped her so much. Mother caught a fever and passed quickly, but father lived ten more months. It seems that his life drained out of him after her mother passed. The apothecary said it was probably his heart. Their passing left a deep hole which at times consumes her – a hole of dark sadness. Her parents were more of a delight to her than she was to them, for they always gracefully accepted her.

Delight Days rushed up the stone steps after climbing the last incline of the road. She had to hurry. Reuben said he would be leaving tonight and she had to get the water, then go to town and buy some food. She desperately wished that Reuben would let her in on his thoughts. His moods seemed to be getting darker. He was so intense and anger was gripping him more frequently. She was so afraid that Reuben was doing something wrong. The talk in town is that he is a thief. There are soldiers coming to Sychar more often. They are looking for someone. Could it be Reuben?

Reuben has been a good man, but lately he is not taking personal responsibility, nor wanting to see Elder Josiah. The Elder has helped Delight Days sort things out in her mind before, so maybe he could help Reuben. Delight Days' fourth husband, Dathan, was always blaming others. He was named after one of the conspirators against Moses and never took personal responsibility. Elder Josiah says their souls can become like the Dead Sea- polluted. A polluted heart needs God's grace. She told Reuben that he is becoming inwardly polluted, but he laughed. "God's grace!" he smirked, "What has God done for you?", he snapped with cold, dark eyes. "God's grace is just an illusion!"

Dealing with his moods had been difficult. Reuben had come and gone as he pleased. In her loneliness, the kind window, Elisabeth, who lives close to the well, had become a good friend. Recently she had died. Delight Days realizes she will miss her kindness. Kindness is always a help when life is so hard. Reuben used to be kinder than he is now. What is on his mind? What is he thinking? Why does he not want to tell me his feelings? Is he afraid?

Lately he is so jumpy, always looking around. It is almost like he is afraid of his own shadow. When Reuben had come into her life, there had been a sense of new beginning, new meaning, with new possibilities. However, lately, Delight Days was not so sure there would be any new beginnings.

The elders are telling everyone that spring is arriving. The warmth of the fire is nice, but it is time to go get water. This spring she feels old. Every spring she tries to see her reflection in the water. She was searching to see if there was any beauty left inside her. She had seen a glimpse of it the other day. Her reflection brought sadness because her face has lost its glow. It is empty, not desirable. It is the time in her life when beauty begins to fade.

Look! There is a flower on the road to the well. Her mother would have said, "Delight Days, always have flowers around you, for flowers add color to the bleak, harshness of life." Father told her, one time, "The colors of flowers are a joy". These thoughts have brought comfort to her mind.

A nagging fear has gripped her heart again. Will Reuben leave? And is he a thief? There is too much loss and lack in her life. All this brings a sadness and a feeling of hopelessness. Is Reuben right when he says, "Where is God's grace?" How is it that she has come to this place, empty and feeling alone? Where is God's grace? Her reflection of today is that heartbreak is the natural habitat of most women.

Before Pilate

It is a simple plan, thought Longinus. Antonio, my trusted soldier, has the gift of language. Because of that fact, he can blend in very well with the locals. Pilate will see the plan's worth. Antonio could play the part very well.

Disguised as a thief, he needs to be aware of where he fits into this plan. He needs to be seen by the local folks. Maybe he will become a part of Barabbas' group. The robberies and killings have been intensifying, even reaching as far as Samaria.

Barrabas has been a scourge, but Longinus thinks this trap will work. To catch a thief, one has to become a thief. With the freedom to set traps in pre-determined towns, Antonio may be seen, and then befriended by someone in Barrabas' camp.

The stars indicate that it is close to time to be let into Pilate's hall. Longinus was thankful that Pilate agreed to see him and hear about this plan. The plan consisted of Antonio disguising himself as a Jewish day laborer. He'll be placed in different towns, like Bethany or Jericho. This will allow him to be in each city on predetermined days. All the soldiers will be aware that any thieves caught will have to stand before Longinus. That way if Antonio is caught then he can see that no harm comes to him. As a day laborer Antonio will interact with men desperate for work. Another soldier will be disguised as a merchant with money so Antonio will rob a fake merchant. This is how Antonio will become known as a thief.

The time had come to stand before Pilate who asks my name. "Longinus, the centurion," I reply. After an hour of explaining the idea, Pilate turns to three of his generals. "You think it might work?" he asks them. When they were dismissed they were implementing the plan with Longinus as the leader of this deception. He had greater authority from Samaria to Jerusalem, and knew it would be a very taxing endeavor. With no time line, the superiors know that this deception could take a long time. Barabbas must be stopped and Longinus is given the task to trap him. Riding toward Bethany, Longinus decides that tomorrow Antonio and the fake merchant will start the plan.

The next evening, at an inn in Bethany, sitting in a dark corner, without a uniform, Longinus' nose is assaulted by the smell of smoke, cooked garlic, and leeks. It is doing very little to overcome the scent of the sweaty bodies of men. He watched the scene unfold and was astonished at how well Antonio melted out of sight. There, in the shadows of the inn, Antonio took the purse. The planted merchant let out a cry, as everyone gathered around to see what was happening. There was a cut purse strap in the hands of the merchant, as he shouted he had been robbed. Antonio swiftly faded into the night.

The Color Returns

This particular day did not start off as being any different, though Reuben had come home last night about midnight. Like all days before, it began with the same old sameness, the same old lack of hope. For a long time, Delight Days had been living with Reuben; or rather, he had been living with her. Looking back, she acknowledges the reasons she allowed him to move into her home. One was her need for protection. The other was fear of being permanently damaged by overwhelming and never ending loneliness.

Now, she was walking, alone, at noon, to the well again. This landmark outside of Sychar, seemed to be the hub of her existence. Because of her multitude of dreary visits to this hole in the earth, it no longer meant anything special--no more meaningful than the dully-colored rocks on the lackluster landscape. Even the waves of heat, shimmering between her and the well, did not fascinate her as they had in the past. The sun was bright and to see the way ahead required squinting her eyes with eyelashes forming a screen of sorts from the glare of the mid-day sun above. The vultures were circling in the sky above her as if waiting for her to die.

Reuben was a desert man and had lately become a very jealous man. Maybe it happened because he was gone all the time. Even though they were not married, Reuben's sense of owning her provoked intense jealousy. He had a fierce fear of being replaced in her life, by some other man. He tried to follow her everywhere, but tried to do it without her knowing it. Men are so foolish to think that women aren't on to their schemes. When Delight Days would ask why he was sneaking around, he would admit it and suggest he was suspicious of what she might do if someone more desirable than he should approach her. So then he was in effect calling her loyalty into question, when the real reason was his sense of being inferior in comparison to other men. His jealousy, at times, was as stifling and suffocating as the hot, blistering winds of summer.

Delight Days never went to the well with the women of the town because they didn't want her around. They couldn't hide it, and she didn't want to pretend to tolerate it. Reuben never could understand that society as a whole had rejected her.

Just last month, Reuben had accused her of having a more than friendly relationship with Elder Josiah. While it was true that Elder Josiah had been close to her dad and the family, she had no desire to develop a relationship with him. Elder Josiah's wife, of many years, had passed away and Reuben was becoming jealous of him. Certainly, her encounters with him could not be taken as evidence of unfaithfulness.

Again, Reuben's jealousy was the cry of an insecure soul. It could be that he was accusing her of something he himself was doing and feeling guilty about. Liars tend to think everyone else is lying, too. Gossips tend to think others are talking about them. Cheaters tend to think their partners are cheating as well. Thinking about this in the hot sun gave her a headache.

Since they were fighting a lot, she had caught sight of Reuben slinking around behind her, keeping watch over his 'possession'. Elder Josiah once said, "Stay away from jealous people. They lose the ability to see things clearly. They see what they expect to see."

Reuben was watching her as she approached the well. "Oh, merciful heavens!" Delight Day thought. There is a man at the well that she didn't recognize. Reuben will assume it is a planned meeting. It would be incredibly stupid to do something since the area around the well is wide open, with nothing to block anyone's view of what is going on there.

Upon arriving at the well, she was stunned that the man spoke to her. It was considered inappropriate for a man to speak to a woman he didn't know.

Another aspect to this was that by his speech, it was obvious that he was a Jew, and that Delight Days was a Samaritan. Jews looked down on Samaritans, and would consider themselves unclean even if they touched something a Samaritan had touched.

At first, Delight Days didn't say anything, as she sat the water pot beside the well. Then something caught her eye--flowers! Their colors were so vivid! In this barren landscape around the well, they really stood out. On her many trips to the well, she had seen a few by the roadside, but not these flowers. She remembered on the previous day, that she had placed the water pot close to the exact spot it was in now, and there had not been anything green, and certainly no flowers! She felt an unfamiliar sensation wash over her. What was happening? Later, she would realize that color was about to return to her life, but at that time, she didn't recall her father's words as he quoted Elder Josiah. "Son, one day, God will send a Messiah. He will be the Flower of all Mankind."

Her father had said to let flowers make her think of the coming Messiah. He will add fragrance and color to meaningless lives. Straightening up, she slowly turned toward the stranger. Is He the Messiah who will bring color into her life?

That is Strange

Delight Days looked at the stranger as he asked her a question. Reuben would be watching from a distance. No doubt there would be a big fight tonight. He is so jealous, and he will probably think this man means something, even though he is nothing to her—a nobody, just another man. So, let Reuben get angry, furious even. She was determined never to talk to this man. She would show Reuben.

Then, she couldn't believe her own ears. She spoke, "Did you say something? You want some water?" He was undoubtedly a Jew, based on how he was dressed. Delight Days thought he might even be a Rabbi, but her father said Rabbis never spoke to a Samaritan, especially a Samaritan woman.

Turning her thoughts back to the reason for being here, she wondered if the water level had dropped. Elder Josiah told her it had never gone dry, but the water had dropped on occasion. Meanwhile, what was she going to do with this man at the well? She told herself to avoid looking at him and just focus on the well as she drew the water. She did this every day. She always tried to get here at the same time, when the sun was directly overhead, thinking maybe one day she could see her reflection in the water.

Her thoughts were coming quickly. Reuben was watching. A Jewish man was talking to her. Does she answer his question? It was then she blurted out, "Why in the world would a Jew ask a Samaritan woman for a drink of water?" It was like she was moving in slow motion, as she gave him a drink of water from a drinking gourd, hanging on the side of the well. After slowly drinking from the gourd, he said, "I can give you living water." He smiled at her, with a smile that almost suggested a bit of humor.

Did she hear him right--Living water? Was this a joke? What is this man trying to do? Was he going to supply her with water that will satisfy her thirst for the rest of her life? That would certainly save a lot of trips to this, or any, well. This man is really different from other men and the way he speaks is very different from how other men usually talk. She decided to go along with him in this strange conversation.

"Sir, you have to be kidding. Look how deep the well is, and you obviously don't have a water pot to draw from it. You are in no position to offer anyone any water, living or not", she said, with a laugh. She continued, "Our father, Jacob, watered his cattle here, his children drank from this well. Living water? What is that? Are you greater than he was?" She looked more closely at the man, and he is still smiling. He didn't seem threatened or insulted by her challenge; he seemed to be enjoying their encounter and was definitely not intimidated.

He directed her attention to the drinking gourd, which still had a little water in it. "If you drink this water, you will thirst after a while. The water I give you will prevent you from ever thirsting again. It comes from a well that bubbles with everlasting life". Delight Days thoughts were blurring in her head. Living water? From what well? Where is it located? Hot days or cold, she would never have this chore to do ever again. Never have to endure the piercing stares of the gawking populace. She couldn't resist the idea. "Sir," she said, "Give me this water. I'm tired of being thirsty."

She quickly glanced over her shoulder to see what Reuben was doing, other than hiding in plain sight. She saw him hiding behind a boundary marker. Looking back at the man at the well, she realized he had followed her glance. His smile was broader than before. "Why not call your husband here before we proceed?" Her mind exploded in six different directions. Like a herd of sheep, fleeing a prowling bear, her thoughts scattered in fear. "Um-my husband? I'm not married!" she blurted out. "I have no husband."

There was much tenderness in his eyes as he said, "You are telling the truth. You have been married five times and you aren't married to the man with whom you are now living."

Her mind froze. Is this man at this well able to read her thoughts, her life's history, all her hurts and sadness? She felt sick to her stomach, realizing that all her life had not been as restricted to her community as she had assumed. How would a common man know this? He must be what her father called "a holy prophet".

She felt the slight breeze. It seemed to cool things down. Was this man a prophet? Father always said there were prophets or holy ones. He had said, "Delight Days, you will know one when you see one." He had always looked for a prophet, but never saw one. Now, can you believe it? Right here, at the well, she may have met a prophet. Father also said that if he met a prophet, he would say, "I realize you are a prophet, so tell me about where we should worship." She seemed to remember that when she next spoke. Her voice was a higher pitch than usual, "My family worships at Mt. Gerazim, but the rabbis say to worship at Jerusalem." She couldn't believe she had the audacity to put a prophet on the spot like that. Is he a prophet or a politician, or an enchanter like Simon?

She was surprised to hear his answer, or at least the way he answered. He did not dismiss her with the tone of his voice, as he replied, "Believe me, the days of only worshiping in Jerusalem or Mt. Gerazim will be replaced with an openness to worship anywhere. Believers will worship the Father in spirit and in truth."

If God is a spirit being why can't you worship him in your spirit, with a desire for truth? Is this prophet at the well saying that truth is the mark of true worship of the Father?

These are new thoughts, but she will never forget his blunt, yet not unkind words, "Salvation is of the Jews". Her mind seemed to be working laboriously, trying to connect and absorb these new thoughts. She could see the logic of his words and see them as truthful.

Her mind went back to another statement of her father's, "If you ever encounter a prophet, you must realize he could be the Messiah." Did she dare to hope? There seemed to be a lifting in her heart that this man at the well might be the Messiah.

Looking into the eyes of this prophet at the well, she had to know. Instead of being the Jew, the man, or the prophet could he actually be the Messiah at the well? As she held her breath for a moment, it felt as if her heart were on fire. She could be on the verge of a momentous experience. Voice trembling, she whispers, "Are you the Messiah? We have been taught that when He comes, He will tell us all things."

The eyes of the prophet at the well seemed to take on an almost fiery glow and his voice had an authority to it that had been absent before as He said, "I am He."

It was as though a shock of energy flowed through her entire body, soul and spirit. She could hardly believe it! She had been having a personal conversation with the Messiah!

Looking back toward Sychar, and then to the Messiah, her heart had a level of joy she had never experienced before. She saw a group of men coming toward the well, from the direction of town, and wondered if they had any idea of the true identity of the man they were going to meet at the well. Reuben had given up and seemed to be walking in the direction of the house and not even trying to hide his presence from her. She needed to tell him the Messiah had come at last. She then realized the town of Sychar needed to be told as well, no matter how they had treated her. She must go quickly! She had found the Messiah!

Delight Days also realized she had left her water pot at the well as she hurried to Sychar. It would keep. The men she passed on the way were twelve in number. Most appeared to be Jewish. As they looked at her, she could sense very little, if any, compassion. It was as though she was nobody to them. Not so with the Messiah. Not only did he look at her, He actually saw her; no, he looked into her, into her soul. His words touched her heart showing a grace she had not experienced before. Strangely, it seemed as if His voice had a musical effect on her heavy heart--a heart that needed to hear tenderness.

Then she saw Reuben! The way he was acting, she knew he was not just angry, he was incensed! He was in a rage! When she caught up to him, she said, "He is the Messiah!" and kept on running.

Delight Days realizes that it is many steps from the well. It seemed longer than usual today in her hurry to tell the townspeople the good news. Entering the town, she ran up to people telling them to "come with me, come quickly! You won't believe this, but I met a man who knows everything about me! This must be the Messiah, doesn't it? He's at the well."

There was so much excitement! All the people raced toward her like a flood, and she just kept repeating, "Come on, the Messiah is at the well!"

Following her, they hurried to the well. Some could not believe that a total stranger could tell her about her life. "Yes, this is the Messiah! He told me all about my life. This has to be the Messiah, so come and see Him."

As the people followed her to the well, her mind rose with a new reflection. Had she found hope? Something that would give her life meaning?

Will He Stay?

When the town people arrived at the well, the twelve men were with the Messiah. She later found out that the twelve were called disciples. Some of the village males said there may be trouble since they were all Jews.

Elder Josiah said, "Delight Days has told us about what has happened. Of all the misfortune that has come her way, she has never lied to any of us, so what she says must be true. That is why we are here."

As Elder Josiah spoke, she felt so overwhelmed by a new round of joy. It was like much of her pain had been replaced by the thought that she could make it because of this man at the well.

Then she heard Elder Josiah invite Him to his house. He said, "Come and teach us at Sychar!" She thought that would be great. The people would be able to talk to Him and understand.

As the thirteen men, and the town's residents moved away from the well, she felt the need to stand there for a while. Somewhere, in her mind, the memory of a long ago thought resurrected itself. Whisper a prayer. She obeyed that thought.

She began to pray, "Adonai, the Messiah told me that now is the time I can worship You in spirit and in truth. This is the day I saw the flowers at the well. Those flowers spoke to me, in a way, telling me that because of the Messiah, I can have color in my life. It almost seems as though Messiah is the flower of my soul. Yes, that is what it seems like. He did not shun me. So much of my life seems like one long shunning experience. Thank you for your grace that accepts me."

As she picked up the water pot, it dawned on her that she still had many steps to go, but her steps now seemed different somehow. She was unable to understand why things seemed so different.

There was so much happening. Many of the important people of Sychar took Messiah's followers into their homes. Elder Josiah had the man at the well stay in his house. What seemed so wonderful was that even I was allowed to come and listen to the Messiah teach. I had hoped that Reuben would come with me to be part of the celebration. Reuben laughed, "You tell me I need God's grace, and now I need to listen to this Messiah. Ha! I don't want anything to do with him!"

The first day, Messiah was busy visiting with the people. It was a strange sight, to see Him and his disciples going from house to house regardless of how humble or nice it might be. Sometimes, Messiah would teach and sometimes one of his disciples would. Always, there was a prayer of blessing on each household.

In the evenings, the entire town would gather to hear him. There was teaching, fellowship, food and fun! He had a tremendous sense of humor. There was more than one side to Him. He was a man who was balanced; not given to extremes of temperament or behavior.

Elder Josiah said that he had never heard anyone, before or since those days, explain the Torah, especially the Book of Deuteronomy, like the Messiah did. In fact, Deuteronomy appeared to be his favorite book. In the cool of the day, all were able to hear the questions the elders put to him. The questions were important and His answers were extremely insightful and opened our eyes to God's truth, teaching us how to live by His Word.

A lot of changes happened during those two days. Many came up to her and said they had heard about her testimony and how she believed the Messiah was genuine. In some ways, her testimony influenced Sychar, but it was the effect of His words that brought about the changes. If He hadn't been who He said He was, anything she could say would be useless. His words became so easy to believe. The most wonderful thing was that His words were the very words of Adonia.

One moment in time that she will never forget took place during the evening of the first day, as she was walking home. Her thoughts were going in all directions. She had listened to His words that day, and suddenly the truth forced her to decide. She wasn't living right.

What is a woman in her position to do? Life had been full of lack, pain and sadness. She had felt that sadness. It seemed so huge that it had a life of its own. In the still of night, it was almost as if sadness had eyes heavy with fear and pain. Fear and pain was how sadness looked at her.

As for Reuben, she has to quit living with him. He will not like it.

Is it possible to ever forget what a person hears the Messiah teach? Those two days helped her see things she had forgotten. A life of lack makes it easy to forget what you should remember. The Messiah had been here for two days. He taught us many things we needed to know about how to live life.

He was powerful in his teaching on faith. He told of a certain village that needed rain, and how they came together and prayed. Only one young boy brought a blanket to cover himself during the rain. That is what faith does. It causes a person to act as if it is going to happen.

It was that loud-talking fisherman who taught a lesson by tossing a baby in the air. The baby laughs because she isn't afraid. She knows he will catch her. That is the attitude we should have in regard to our Heavenly Father. Trust Him.

Then Messiah told about a farmer who planted his seeds, and worked the ground. The labor is hard, but he does it. Those seeds will have their own lives. Their lives will give life to the eater. The hope is in the harvest. The farmer gets up and works the land. His hope is in the life in the seeds. That hope causes him to work the ground until the harvest comes. Hope is transforming.

The Messiah had a lot to say about our future. He tried to instill in all of us, the right place to put our trust. Trust in the Father comes from faith. Trust and faith gives us hope. Oh, what a great Teacher! He inspired hope in us. He brought us into a deeper level of knowledge. Hope looks to the future. Hope gives confidence. Hope and confidence create peace. Her mind had been opened to so many new truths. These truths seemed to bring peace to her heart. She remembered the words of the Messiah, "My peace I give to you."

Those two days were different, not only for her, but for all Sychar. It seemed that the Messiah dealt with what should govern one's heart--love God, love your neighbor.

Growing Children

The man at the well would be leaving in the morning. The last night of the Messiah's visit to Sychar, was coming to an end. He had preached about the Kingdom of Heaven. It was great! Elder Josiah had invited all who wanted to come, to do so. Even she was invited! Her childhood friend told Delight Days that she could go to the meeting and also to the well with the other women in the morning.

Meeting the man at the well had changed her life. It seemed that her life had taken on a new identity. She could not explain it, but there was definitely something different.

That night, after most had gone home, she realized it was time for her to leave as well. Suddenly, the man from the well came around the corner of the house, with eight young children in tow. Surprised by the sight of the children around him, she asked if she could help take care of them. "It would be helpful if you would hold the baby boy," he answered with a smile. She laughs about it now, as she thinks about how she'd never been a mother, but here she was watching a baby.

Sitting down, He gathered the children close to Him. Slowly, and lovingly, He began to speak. First, He placed his hands on Avery's head. His prayer of blessing seemed to touch her. Softly, He asked the Father to touch her heart. He said, "She feels very deeply. This bend in her personality can be a blessing of joy or a source of heartache and pain. Help her to always feel deeply and desire Godly thoughts so she can help others," he prayed.

Then he reached out to Jude, placing one hand on Jude's head while looking into his eyes. Messiah then said, "Father, here is a little lamb that has it in his heart to be a peacemaker. The world could use more who walk in peace and bring it to their fellow men."

Shifting to his side, he placed his hand on Micah. "Father, here is a young man who has a heart of a warrior. May he use that heart full of strength and determination to fight for Truth."

Smiling at Rori and Beckett, He placed one hand on each of their heads and prayed. "Heavenly Father, here is a young girl who loves to have friends. May she always be a friend to those who are abused and broken. And Father, may this young man, Beckett, who is all boy, maintain his inquisitive nature. His mind runs to curiosity and wanting to learn. May he always have a great curiosity to learn about his heavenly Father."

Reaching out, he placed a hand on Ella's head. "Father, Ella likes to help. Enable her to balance that desire by showing Your love when she helps others Father, and may she aid many who are hurting in life. She has a heart to love."

"Father, Violet has the fragrance of laughter. May her smile inspire others to hope in Your love. May her sense of enjoying life always be a part of her life that she shares with others."

Reaching for the baby in my arms, He took the infant into His own and prayed, "Father, this baby is Sparrow. May he be aware that you always have your eyes on the sparrow. You always see their needs and care about them. Help Sparrow grow up, knowing You are watching over him."

Those prayers of blessing the Messiah prayed over the children will never leave her mind. However, the prayer that touched her most was the prayer He prayed blessing her. He asked His Father to aid her in finding the courage to walk in newness of life.

As she lifted her eyes to Him, tears were streaming down her face. But as she looked into His eyes, she saw a tear. That tear affirmed her personhood. She had value to Him. "Thank you" was all she could say, as the parents came to get their children.

The next morning, as thirteen men passed by her hut, she heard them singing softly. As she went outside, the Messiah turned toward her and said something very curious, "Delight Days, watch for a bee". Then He walked on.

At mid-day, walking to the well, her mind was reflecting on two things. First, it seemed that the Messiah had helped many to find acceptance. Why and how she couldn't say. But these two days showed her how much the Messiah accepted others. He accepted her! What a wonderful experience of grace.

Her mind also rose into the troubled waters of Reuben. How would or could he find the Messiah's grace?

Reuben

The day after the man at the well left, Delight Days was walking the last forty feet toward the little hut, but she had to be honest with herself. Did she love Reuben? Was he to be part of her life anymore? This little hut had become her home. Trying to make it work with Reuben, surviving by foraging for food after the harvest, getting water, trying to eliminate lack in life. Is this what life had become?

There had been some men. She knew it was wrong. How does this happen? Men love and leave. Some stay longer than others, but they leave. Reuben knew her story. She had been with him for a year and a half- 447 days, after all. But lately, it seemed that Reuben was becoming more and more remote. He had moved away from caring about her feelings and needs. That was it! He had become more self-centered. He had become a person who only thought about himself. He had become consumed with anger and jealousy.

That old hut had served as a shelter for her. She had tried to fix it up all she could; then there was Reuben, standing in the pitiful doorway. She couldn't believe it. Reuben just looked at her. She wanted to tell him all that the Messiah had to share, but he just stood there looking into her eyes. Then, with a whisper of a voice, he said, "I see you have a new friend."

In disbelief, all she could say was, "Really? Really?"

Did he really think she had a new boyfriend?

"No!" her mind screamed. "He is the Messiah. He is someone Who can speak to the heart. The One Who can break the dry thought that comes to the human soul, due to lack. He is not a boyfriend."

There it was again! That intense look of anger--that glaring anger! Reuben reached out and grabbed her, pulling her arm behind her. The pain was sharp. There was total rage in his mind, at that point, and he was going to hurt her. She cried out, in her mind, "Help me, Adonai!"

That moment seemed to stand still. She can't explain it, but it seemed as if some type of peace just came over her. It was as though she had been in a storm that suddenly calmed. Whatever had happened seemed to put a resolve in her heart. There she was, bone weary, due to the last few days' activities, not the weariness of a troubled mind, but a good kind of weariness.

You could almost smell his anger. You could definitely see it. Reuben wanted to lash out, to hit. Elder Josiah always said, "There are those who allow their jealousy to strike out."

Reuben, in his rage, hit her in the pit of her stomach, like a battering ram. She couldn't breathe, and her eyes started to roll back from the pain as the water pot crashed to the floor. Reuben stood over her, just glaring. He screamed, "I am done with you!" On her knees, trying to catch her breath, she watched Reuben walk away. She wept on the floor, from both the physical and emotional pain.

Summer's End

It was like no spring she had ever experienced, the spring she met the man at the well. Before that spring, there had been no spring in her soul. No future, no hope. It had been hard and next to impossible really, to see any good in her life.

Now, the end of summer had arrived. She had spent a lot of time trying to make sense of all that had transpired. Elder Josiah said it seemed everyone had been able to find a way to apply something to their life after those two days. He called it "Redemption". It is so hard for her to explain her inward feelings. All is new--a new reality.

There seems to be truth in Elder Josiah's words. "The encounter with the man at the well was redemptive." Her prayers had even taken a different direction. They were addressed to the "Heavenly Father, in the name of, with the authorization of, the Messiah". Redemption had taken her out of the pit of despair. Maybe despair is where a person is doomed by the anxiety of sameness; same loss, same lack and the same longing. Emotionally, life seemed to take on an air of adventure, a journey of new hope and direction.

Those two days seemed to divert her from focusing on a lot of tragedies of her own making. His voice was echoing in her mind, "Go and stop sinning. Be passionate about God."

Through the months there has been a birth of resilience in her. She's able to handle life better because it seems He is still with her.

Whatever is happening, she may not be able to explain because she doesn't fully understand it, but here is what she knows: In being discarded by society, she found the Messiah, and He accepted her. Yes, in the morning, she will get up and not feel like a...a.... what word does she choose? A loser!

It's funny how thoughts come back that you haven't thought of in a long time. Is that a normal thing, or is it somehow wrong? She was remembering how Father had made a path by the house, and he walked it almost every day. He placed stones to help him remember things that needed to be remembered. He said a person can easily forget, even important things or sayings. Each stone represented a thought he had learned.

Well, Delight Days made her own path of stones to remind her of some important items she didn't want to forget. The man at the well said a lot of things during those two days, which she believed were very important to remember.

The first stone was what Delight Days called the "well stone". She carried a small stone to the side of her hut, and placed it gently but firmly on the hard soil. It represented the well, where she met Him, and where her life began to change.

There is a stone about the love of Adonai and a stone of prayer. One stone she placed that was difficult for her was the stone of forgiveness--forgiving those who have wronged her. She had so much hurt, so much lack, so much disappointment.

These stones will help her stop and remember His words. In fact, it was her grandfather who gave her father the idea of placing stones. He told her father how the Israelites placed stones as a monument to remind them of the miracle that took place when they crossed the Jordan River. She had never seen that river. Grandfather said he had. When he went there, on his return, he brought a stone back to remind him what God had done.

Delight Days' father and grandfather both said that Sychar would be a better place if people would remember. "People are too focused on life, "he said, "Because God has been forgotten. Always have something that helps you remember." For her it was rocks.

So that is why she has placed rocks. Those rocks help her remember His words. Oh, she even placed a rock that reminds her to "watch for a bee".

Fall

It's been over seven hundred days since she met the man at the well. Every once in a while, someone will hear some news about him. One said He walked on top of the waters of Lake Gennesaret. Another told Elder Josiah that He fed over five thousand people by increasing a small lunch, to more than enough to take care of everyone there. Still others reported that He's preaching and healing are amazing people.

To be honest, her encounter with Him has made her a better person. Maybe all those He is encountering will be changed as well. Hmmm... What was the bee business? Why would she need to watch out for a bee?

Suddenly, a bee seemed to be trying to get her attention. All right, she'll follow the bee. Unlike most bees she's crossed paths with, this bee was flying comparatively slower. When she thought she lost him, he came back! This was more than odd! She was heading north of the hut, but why would the bee head in that direction? There were not many flowering plants in that direction, but the man at the well did tell her, as He left town, "watch for a bee".

Then the bee left and didn't come back. Was there something she was supposed to do? Did she follow the wrong bee? Suddenly she felt impressed to go home and come back tomorrow.

For the next three days, she followed the bee every way he flew. He would guide her up to a certain point, and then speed up and disappear. Those four days were exciting. She would need to glean the fields soon, but she was told to watch the bee, so watch the bee she did. These days of her bee journey had been fun. Hopefully, the harvest will be better this season, and maybe she'll be able to locate the bee again.

That will definitely be a miracle. Everyone else seemed to be able to locate beehives, but she had no experience or teaching on how to do so. Hey! What if she could locate the honey her father called "amber gold?

Each day she would leave the hut and go in a different direction. She always took a different route to where she last saw the bee. Then, one morning, as she came to the last location she had seen the bee, there it was! That's when she approached a small mound of rocks that seemed to create a natural hive.

As she walked around the hive, she was wondering how to harvest the honey. Maybe it was a miracle, maybe not. What she believed, with all her heart, is that the man at the well worked it out. Here it was!

Then she noticed a small opening on the back of the rocky hive. As she reached her finger into the crack, she thought, "This probably isn't the most rational thing to do," but there she was, doing it anyway. When she had examined the area with her finger, and removed it, it was covered with the amber gold!

Walking quickly back to her hut, she wondered how to handle this blessing. If she brings someone to help her, she would probably lose most of the honey. There were some people in Sychar who would tell people about it. One thing she could do would be to place a pot right under where the honey was, leaking out and it could fill the pot overnight. Maybe she could come back every two days.

She could go to the wheat harvest and glean, but at night, go to the hive and change out the small pots. Yes, this fall would be a blessed fall for her. She'll glean and collect the amber gold.

Following the Rabbi

Antonio realizes that the Rabbi is walking again. The crowd was not huge, but a fair amount of people. Those twenty to twenty-five people were listening like me.

It was after the Rabbi started walking that the young rich ruler showed up. He wants to know how to go to heaven. It is at that moment that Antonio sees Reuben. He's not one hundred percent sure that Reuben is the thief of Samaria, but when Longinus sees him, he will know. He is the one who got a look at the thief many months ago.

Antonio can deal with Reuben. Watching, he can see that he's going to rob the young man of his purse. Hearing the words of this Rabbi has touched Antonio's heart as never before. "How long have I been listening?" Antonio says to himself. Not even thirty minutes. Strange, it is as if his words have some type of power. It is almost like whatever this rabbi says explodes in his heart. It seems his words are important. There is fire in them.

When the rich young ruler started talking to the Rabbi, it became very quiet. It was strange. Even the dogs quit barking. Who is this Rabbi? He is so different that he decides he will follow Him for a while.

Reuben can't believe it! This young ruler has just walked up to a man. It is the man from the well. Delight Days said grace was in this man's words and actions. This man is not some great person. Seeing this man makes his mind go to those times with Delight Days. One thing is for sure, He changed her. It was like she became a new person. Now the young ruler is trying to impress this man at the well.

Reuben remembers what Delight Days had told him. His heart was dark and his life will go downhill if he walks away now. She had asked him not to leave, but there had been a great restlessness within him. He didn't care for anyone or anything lately. But, that day seemed to drive him away. He remembers it so well.

That was the day when the man at the well showed up. Delight Days got so excited. "I found the Messiah," she said. Going about from house to house, she was telling everyone, "I found the Messiah". He is going to stay and teach, so let us go hear him, Reuben", she babbled.

The whole town had to be simpletons. Don't they know they are charlatans in every place? Have they not heard of Simon the Sorcerer? He says he is a god. So, now is this Jew a God? As Reuben laughed, he thought people would believe anyone who said they can give hope.

His experiences in life have no room for hope, only money. Hope cannot buy bread but money can. Becoming a thief had made it easier to get money. The quickest and easiest way is to find an inn. Look, there is a merchant. He is a fool. He thinks no one will rob him. Reuben follows him. Walking past him one can see he is a young ruler, one of those who has enough money to buy influence and honor. He thinks to himself, "This young ruler will pay for my supper tonight." Money is my grace, not God, he thought as he hurriedly followed the young ruler.

Hold it! Is that Antonio? He has watched this thief steal. He's standing behind those people. He is a good thief, but not as good as Reuben. Every once in a while, Reuben hears whispers of Antonio in the inns.

This is strange. Antonio seems to be listening to the conversation. The ruler just asked how one can go to heaven. What a misguided bunch of people. Circling closer to the young ruler, Reuben can see his purse.

Did he hear right? The man at the well just told him to go and sell all and give to the poor. "Boy, that's great!" thought Reuben, "I am the poor and I am the one who needs this rich ruler's purse."

In watching the crowd moving closer to what is being said, it seems that Antonio is also focused on the conversation. All at once, the rich young ruler turns and walks away. He just rejected what the man from the well said. This rich young ruler is like Reuben—money is his grace, not heaven.

Well, he's going to see how hard it is to live without money because Reuben plans on relieving him of his. Looking back around, he sees the thief, Antonio, following the man from the well. Smiling broadly, he reaches the corner just as the rich young ruler walks in the bend. Bumping into him, his hands cut the leather strap that holds the moneybag. He's too shocked to realize what Reuben just did. Before he bumps into him, Reuben looks into his eyes. Those were the saddest eyes he has ever seen.

Passover

Passover was approaching. The man at the well had made it clear that Jerusalem was the proper place to worship Passover. The Samaritans worshipped on Mt. Gerazim. This tension about where to worship had existed for centuries between the Jews and Samaritans.

Delight Days remembered how uncomfortable Messiah made her people feel about His Jewish positions. Ever since He arrived, the people had talked about going to Jerusalem for Passover. That would be an adventure no one would ever forget. My grandfather and father had both been to Jerusalem, which is admittedly a great city.

Elder Josiah said if anyone wanted to go, they could travel with a caravan that was coming through Sychar. It would cost each person 20 shekels, which would be paid to the caravan master.

Selling the amber gold allowed her to have enough money to go to Jerusalem. Safety was very much on her mind in joining together within a caravan. When she told Elder Josiah she would like to go, he responded by saying he always knew she would, since she wanted to hear the man from the well teaching again.

The first day of the trip was a warm day. The caravan master was a kind man. The walk of forty miles would not be hard. They could travel that distance in about four days, no more than four days and a half. That would put them in Jerusalem on Thursday, just before Passover.

Excitement ran high in Delight Days' heart. Most of the village had not heard of what she was doing--a woman traveling to Jerusalem? But, as Elder Josiah said, "The man at the well changed so many things."

The town was encouraging to her as she left. Three years earlier, she couldn't even have imagined their acceptance of her.

The well had become her friend; the bee had become her friend. These experiences in Delight Days' life have led her here. Where is "here"? On the road to Jerusalem! Can you imagine a Samaritan being excited about that? It was unheard of! Physically, she was tired, but spiritually motivated and that kept her going. Fortunately, she even had enough money to buy bread, cheese and dates. She couldn't remember the last time she had cheese. Oh yes, it was during those two days, when everyone in Sychar came to hear the Messiah. She had even brought a small pot of honey, in case she needed to sell it.

The journey was a time to reflect on the goodness of Adonia. More and more, she was embracing the Jewish writings. The man at the well told all of them in Sychar that salvation was from the Jews. Their Holy Book is much more than their Samaritan Pentateuch. It seemed to give more insights.

At last, the caravan master said they would see the city over the next hill. She moved closer to the front. Wow! The sight Delight Days saw made her come to a complete stop. She just stood there looking at that great city. Jerusalem was nothing like she had imagined it! It was far more than her mind could comprehend! Her grandfather and father's eyes had seen it and now she was seeing it! If you get a chance to see for yourself, you will understand.

There are so many sights: different kinds of dress, different races of people, and different types of Jewish faith, like Sadducees and Pharisees. The caravan master told her to be careful of these people. They love to condemn. They were not at all like the man from the well, who accepted her. It is said that Passover brings people from all over the world – Jews, who live outside of Israel. This will be a good day. Now is the time to find the man at the well.

So, where is "here"? Is it at Jerusalem? This moment will be full of hope when she will again experience the man at the well. "Here" is now. "Here" is the present. "Here" is grace.

Jerusalem – Spring

It wasn't until after three on Thursday afternoon that Delight Days was finally able to leave the caravan. The past few days had been wonderful for her. She was out of Sychar, and meeting new people. Even some of the people in the caravan had befriended her. Now she was in the city of Jerusalem.

Due to the lateness of the hour, the caravan master cautioned her to stay with the caravan, but she had come too far to stay put. She decided to keep trying to find the man from the well. Surely, He has to be by the temple. Someone had to know this man. After all, He is the Messiah.

So far Delight Days had found only a few who knew of this Messiah on the streets. "Who is this Messiah?" some asked. Others questioned if He was the miracle worker they had heard about.

As she looked down the narrow, winding street, she began to see what looked like shadows, forming on the road. Soon, it will be dark. It was getting later, the crowds were getting thicker, and it was getting difficult to push through them. She heard someone say the gates of the city were slowing the flow of people. As she pushed and shoved her way through the mass of people, she realized how wrong this was--to expose herself in a strange city in a time of uproar such as this.

The shadows were coming faster now, and soon the people in the Temple would be leaving to head for the Passover meals. She wanted so much, to make it to the Temple, but she knew she needed to head back to the caravan for her safety. There was nowhere to spend the night. She hadn't given any thought as to how challenging it would be to get to the Temple.

Walking uncertainly through the labyrinth of streets, she thought, "This is another night of disappointment. I want to see the man from the well again--to hear Him teach. Here it goes again--another disappointment! I'm sure the man at the well never experienced any disappointment!"

It must be fantastic to live as the man from the well does, with all the praise from everyone, because everyone loves him. All are glad to see Him. No one would ever reject Him, would they? At that moment, Delight Days had forgotten that not everyone in Sychar accepted Him, as her mind recalled Reuben's rejection.

Finally, she saw the face of the caravan master, smiling, as always. He welcomed her back. He seemed sincerely relieved that she was safe. As she sat by his fire, she overheard him talking about the crowd and how hard it was to get through Jerusalem. Sitting there, in the fading light, Delight Days asked herself if she was on a fool's journey. Should she have stayed at home? The caravan master brought her some food to eat, and encouraged her to eat it. She had been so caught up in her search for the Messiah that she had forgotten to eat. The caravan master said, "Eat first, and then we will talk."

The food was warm and flavorful. She looked from time to time, at the caravan master's face. He didn't look like a Jew or a Samaritan, but he was very familiar with the Passover celebration. He told me that his people are not worshipers of my Adonai. About midway through their conversation, he asked, no, almost commanded, her to tell him about the man she called the man from the well. He was somewhat shocked by her reaction. Delight Days could hardly believe what came out of her mouth. Her thoughts were racing, like a mountain stream, as she went from thought to thought, in quick succession. As she shared about the man from the well, she gazed overhead to the stars and realized one thing.

What Delight Days realized was that she could not stop. Everything came out about her life: her father, Elder Josiah, her husbands, Reuben, meeting the man at the well, the two days, her hurts, her lacks, her disappointments. He listened attentively to them all. When Delight Days finished, she just sat quietly, looking at the fire. It felt like all that talking had just about taken the last of her energy. Finally, he spoke. He said, "Thank you." Had a man ever said those words to her? If so, she couldn't remember it. He continued, "Thank you for explaining how you have found what all people want. Someone to believe in, to hope in."

What had become an afternoon of disappointment, had turned into a night of acceptance. Why, or how, had it happened? Delight Days decided it was because the man at the well was worth talking about.

How Did it Happen?

Rachel had been on Reuben's mind a lot lately. He remembered that it was she that told him to watch out for Antonio. It has been some time since he had left Delight Days and he and Rachel had been together, mainly because she worked at the inn of Bethlehem.

"Antonio is not what he seems", she said. "He comes to the inn here but he only spends his money for a meal. Most thieves gather a few men around them."

Thinking about Antonio, he had a question. It seemed that no one knew those who Antonio had robbed. On two occasions Reuben had seen him steal, but he didn't know who the victims were. He is good, but never as smooth as himself.

It is said that he is always asking about Barabbas. Why that was Reuben didn't know, but he did know he would never tell where Barabbas was. One does not just walk in and demand to see Barabbas. His name has been whispered for years, yet few know who he is. Even fewer know where he is staying.

Reuben stops and listens. Why didn't he stop sooner? The dogs were barking, so he didn't think anyone could hear him. According to the stars, it is getting close to midnight.

He had sensed the last three nights that he was being followed, but he wasn't sure. Barabbas always said not to come if he thought he was being followed. There is the faint whiff of cooked food and smoke. It is faint, but he realizes that he's close to Barabbas' house. His ears pick up a faint sound. Is someone tracing his steps?

Stopping in mid stride, he hears the sound of rocks being moved by a footfall, or what sounds like footfalls. Reuben waited ten minutes on the dusty road before he quickened his steps. Ahead is where Barabbas is staying. One can make out a single sliver of light from inside the hut. All of those who work under him meet at certain times and tonight was his night to meet. Barabbas' strategy for robbing has kept the Romans at bay for years. This way, everyone has a place to be in different cities.

Anticipating meeting with him in a few minutes, he hears barking dogs a few streets over. It will be hard to hear now, if someone is following, and stopping and looking behind will not do him any good. The stars are hidden now, by deep cloud cover.

Suddenly, a hand grips his arm tightly, with the idea of capture. A slight voice says, "If you make a sound, I will cut your throat." Reuben can feel the sharpness of the blade, as a warm trickle of blood begins to run down his neck. This man, whoever he is, is very skilled. In that moment, his heart and mind both suddenly freezes. No thought of escape enters his thoughts, as his mind holds nothing but emptiness and an inability to think.

A rough voice asks softly, "Are you the thief of Samaria?" Nodding, he hears the low whistle of a night bird. From down the street, a faint sound is heard and in less than a minute, he's being dragged back up the street to a band of soldiers. His eyes begin to adjust to the torchlight. With a shock of horror on his face, he sees the centurion whose camp he had run into. Smiling, he says, "Cry out, and you die."

As shouts ring out from down the street, it dawns on Reuben that he was the one who led them to Barabbas. Just then, two bound men are thrust into his presence. Behind them comes the thief, Antonio, wearing a soldier's uniform. It was he that deceived Reuben and he was very good at it. He had led Antonio to Barabbas.

As Reuben is thrust into the jail, he comes face to face with Elsi, the chief jailer. He has been entrusted to watch over Barabbas and his band. He tells us he is to prepare three crosses. Two of them will be for the thieves. The third one will be for the one who calls Himself King of the Jews. This is to take place soon, for the Jewish Holy Day of Passover is close. He has never tried to understand the Passover concept. To the Jews, it is important to their meaning to life. Reuben hears Elsi say it is his appetite is what gives him meaning in life. He laughs quietly. It is known he loves hard wine and women.

Reuben is down on himself. He is afraid of both Barabbas and Jehoram. They know he led the thief Antonio to where Barabbas was. The truth is Antonio has been following Reuben for the past three nights. Longinus had put together a great plan, with Antonino catching over twenty thieves in these past thirty months.

As the night moves into morning, Longinus comes and tells Elsi to bring Barabbas, Reuben and Jehoram to Pilate's Hall. There Pilate will pronounce judgment. This being close to the Passover time, Reuben is told there will be a prisoner released causing all three prisoners to wonder who it will be. There seems to be something happening, more activity than normal.

Later Barabbas is led out of Pilate's Hall. Longinus tells Barabbas that his men will take him outside the city. He is to be the prisoner that is set free. He informs him that if they ever see him, in any of the cities of Judea, he will be caught and killed. Quickly Barabbas flees into the labyrinth of streets that crisscross the city of Jerusalem.

Jerusalem – Friday

Did she ever sleep! It was later than Delight Days had slept in years. It was two hours past sun up. The caravan master had laid some food by her bed; well, by her pallet, outside on the ground. In addition, he had bundled up food for later in the day. Delight Days was grateful and moved by his generosity. "Eat, eat, and go! I'll have young Caleb go with you. He has been to the Temple before. If the man at the well is there, Caleb will make sure you get to see Him."

Her experience on this day was far different than the day before. Caleb knew the streets, and they seemed to make good time. He took routes, completely different from the ones she had taken yesterday. Walking down a crowded street, she heard someone say the word "Messiah". She stopped and looked around to see if she could figure out who had spoken. The voice had been that of a woman, and she saw two women near her, so she listened. Delight Days listened to them converse in a way she thought wasn't obvious. What was obvious was that they were talking about the man at the well.

When they paused in their conversation, Delight Days took a step toward them, and asked, "Did you say Messiah?" They looked at her with surprised expressions, back at each other, then at her again, as they stepped back a step, and moved closer to each other. They were obviously suspicious. "What is it to you?" asked the elder of the two, with unveiled suspicion, bordering on malice. "I want to see Him, and I thought He would be at the Temple", she replied.

Laughing, the younger one said, "So you don't know!"

"Know what? Please tell me," Delight Days asked.

"Last night, they arrested a man who calls himself the "Son of God". They had a trial during the night. As the trial was going on, there were some people standing near a fire, outside, where they were holding court."

"Go on, please", she asked softly.

"Up walked a big man, and I said to him, 'You must be a follower of that man on trial'. He looked as if he was scared – no terrified would be the word- terrified. Since I have been around the Galilean, I recognized the accent and he was definitely a Galilean. A lot of this so-called Son of God's followers are Galileans. I mean, what are the chances a Galilean would just happen to start hanging around court that night? I didn't buy what he was telling, you know. The people weren't through with him, and another girl demanded to know if he was a follower of this so called Messiah. He denied it again, with his voice quivering. I left for a few minutes, but when I came back, a guy named Asher, who had a group of people with him, asked the same thing I had. They wanted to know if he was one of the disciples of the King of the Jews."

At this point, she laughed in a cynical way. "Anyway, the big man started calling down curses on himself, like 'May I be struck with leprosy, if I ever knew him or ever even heard of Him!' At that point, he heard the crowing of a rooster, as the sun came up. For some reason, he went from mad to sad, in an instant. He looked around him like a cornered beast, and took to running away as fast as he could. I have never seen a man that size move that quickly! Oh, and he was crying as he ran. I don't mean weeping. I mean he was sobbing. It's strange hearing a man cry."

Delight Days was trembling as she thought she knew who the man was. It had to be the one they called 'Peter'. It's hard for me to believe he has denied his master. Why would he do that? "Quick! Tell me more."

The older woman looked straight into my eyes and said something that chilled me to the bone.

"Well, they are crucifying him, at this very moment."

"Tell me where," she said in a voice barely above a whisper. She couldn't make sense of what she was hearing. The Messiah was arrested? Peter, who was the most vocal of the group, denied even knowing Him? Someone was having Him crucified? Her mind was screaming, "What was happening? Has the whole world lost its mind?"

Grabbing young Caleb by the arm, she asked the two women, "Where is He being crucified?"

The elder of the two women growled, "Oh, let them kill him. He's just a rabble rouser! Everywhere He goes, He stirs up controversy among the people."

At that point, she could stand it no more! Delight Days screamed, "Where is He?"

She pointed to a street nearby. "Take that street and it will take you out of the city. It won't take long for you to see the hill. If somehow you get lost, it's called 'the Place of the Skull'."

Running, she drug Caleb by his arm. Tears blurred her vision. She was bumping into people, stumbling over the uneven ground of the street. As she broke through the crowd she came upon a horrendous scene.

Jerusalem- Golgotha

Nearing the obscene spectacle of the three people being executed, she was gripped with panic. It had been a long time since she felt like she could not breathe. This could not be happening! She didn't come to Jerusalem to see a sight like this! Her insides quivered with the need to vomit. Her head was about to burst with dizziness and she felt her legs beginning to lose their ability to hold her up. "I never should have come!" she thought. Yet, here she was at another disappointment! Again! How horrible to be present at all this disarray, dismay and disorder! It doesn't make sense! If the man on the center cross was the same man she met at the well, then the man at the well wasn't the Messiah, the Christ. Whoever he was, and whatever his intentions, or sincerity, he wasn't the One we had been looking for. All of us have been fooled, whether Jew or Samaritan!

Moving forward to take in what was really happening, Delight Days could only feel dread. She walked as if she were drunk or dying. The only dream Delight Days had believed that could really change her world, and the lives of all people on earth, was now a nightmare! She could see that whoever was on the center cross had been through a brutal experience. Looking closely at his face, I couldn't tell who he was. His face was cut, swollen twice its size, his mouth hung open, so his tongue was lifelessly hanging out. There was so much blood, I couldn't tell if he even had any teeth.

She pointed to the center cross and asked a nearby Roman soldier, with an anxious pressure in her chest, "Is that the one who said He is the Messiah?"

She nearly fainted, as she heard him reply, in a strange, quiet voice, "Yes".

Delight Days asked the same soldier who the people were at the foot of the cross.

"Oh, those are the chief people. They are the ones who worked to kill Him."

At that point, she heard one of those chief people address the crowd who had gathered to see three men die.

"He said he came to seek and save people. That's funny. This Messiah can't even save himself!"

Others in the crowd sneered at him and said, "He said He was the Chosen of God. Ha!"

Her mind wanted her to scream, "He is the Son of God! Who else could He be?" But it was as though she was frozen and could not respond.

As this horrific scene continued, a burly Roman yelled, "If you are the King of the Jews, save yourself!"

This was all so confusing! Were they really crucifying the Messiah? Even at her worst time, she would never do this to a man like the one she met at the well! Why were these men doing this? Surely he is the Messiah! He has to be! Her whole life had changed because of him. What is happening?

The Roman soldier, who had been so kind and helpful, in a difficult circumstance, shushed her, and said, "Listen! Those two thieves are saying something!" One of them was giving the man at the well a hard time, just like the spectators who were mocking him. He challenged the King of the Jews to rescue Himself and the other thieves if He was the Messiah!

The debate between the two dying criminals caught the attention of the crowd and a hush came over all of them. They seemed to be holding their collective breath.

What! She couldn't believe what happened next. She heard a familiar voice, from her past. The voice of Reuben! Oh, Reuben! Why didn't you stay? Why didn't you accept that the man at the well was the Messiah? You chose not to believe!

"Listen", he said to his partner in crime. "We are getting what we have coming to us!" He groaned in pain and then continued, "This man hasn't done anything bad."

The next words have continued to ring in Delight Days mind, over and over.

"Lord, remember me when you come into your kingdom!"

Jesus told Reuben that he would join him in Paradise today!

Moving up closer to the cross in the center, she stood looking up into the eyes of the man at the well. They were nearly closed but she saw a slight nod of recognition. Even at this time, this excruciating time, He knew her! She turned to face the cross from which Reuben was hanging. She searched his face for a sign of recognition. Suddenly, she saw a look of astonishment. His throat, now completely dry, left him unable to speak. He was trying to say something. He was struggling to move his lips. Then he was able to move them. No words were heard, but he clearly mouthed the words, "I'm sorry. I want you to know I have found God's grace". Tears now overwhelmed Delight Days. Two men, over seven hundred days ago had touched her life. One knocked her down with pain, while the other lifted her up with kindness. Each had affected her: one with viciousness, one with virtue. She reflected on the man at the well giving her forgiveness many days ago. The other gave no mercy or forgiveness. Now here forgiveness is given to Reuben.

Looking back, she knew other things were said that day, but now, they were just a blur. She does remember, at about noon, when she was dizzy with questions about all that day, the sun went black, as though Heaven itself was closing its eyes to what was happening. Delight Days thought that very thing as the sky turned black. In the darkness of that moment, tears rushed down her face. "What is happening?" screamed her soul.

Jerusalem – Friday Evening

There was much movement around the center cross. Passover was coming, but Jesus had already died, so His body was being taken away. At that point, the soldiers, in view of the High Holy Day of Passover, were speeding up the deaths of the prisoners by breaking their legs. They would suffocate more quickly. At first, the cracking of leg bones made her jump. When she was told what it was, she covered her ears. Reuben died soon after.

A lady by the name of Ruth came up to her then and said, "John saw you and recognized you. He came up to me and whispered to me that you were the woman at the well. We, who traveled in Christ's circle, know about your story. Jesus told many people about you. It's getting late, and you should come home with me."

Delight Days' emotions were raw, her mind whirling in a million directions. She didn't know what to do. Ruth noticed that she kept looking at Reuben's body. "You know him also, don't you?" she asked.

Delight Days whispered, "Yes."

Tenderly, Ruth placed her arms around her, as she burst into tears.

How long she held her, she didn't know. When no more tears would come, she still held her. Finally, she gently told Delight Days to come with her. Like a person with no will, she let Ruth guide her away. With a weak whisper, I asked, "What about Reuben?"

Ruth replied that the soldiers would see that he is placed in Kidron Valley. Delight Days asked her if that is where Jesus will be buried. Ruth said that he would be buried in a tomb belonging to a member of the Sanhedrin. She felt strongly that they needed to get to her home as soon as possible, so she told Caleb, who had stood by her during the whole terrible time, to tell the caravan master that Delight Days will see him on Monday morning, which is when he plans to leave.

Ruth was a wonderful woman. That night, in spite of both women being worn out, they talked into the wee hours of the morning. Ruth did most of the talking, explaining what she knew of the man from the well.

Staying with Ruth turned into three days and nights. Delight Days knew she would have to leave on Monday, by the third hour, which is 9 A.M.

They talked about all the things the Man at the well had done – all the good He brought into this ugly world. Well, it was ugly in the sense that people would not accept Him as the Messiah.

That Sunday morning, one day before Delight Days would head home, became a day of great hope. Ruth was excited, and came running into the house, saying the Messiah was alive. Everywhere she went, the story was being told. Messiah had come out of the grave!

As the day lengthened, there was so much excitement! If He is the Messiah, then surely He can come out of the grave.

Jerusalem – Monday

This was the day after the Resurrection everyone was talking about. The day the man at the well came back to life! What a difference a few days can make. Of course not all believe, but Delight Days realizes she does! Thinking about all the accounts Ruth shared with her, how could she not believe He came back.

There was much she didn't understand, she told Ruth, as she walked with her to the caravan. Once there, they hugged and cried. Ruth was a real blessing to Delight Days! She was a sweet, gentle person, who reflected the love of Christ!

As they walked, Ruth asked Delight Days what was the main difference she had experienced in her life because of the Man at the well. Delight Days responded by saying that before she met the Man at the well, there was a feeling of total hopelessness and sadness in her life. Meeting the Man at the well was like finding hope. Then, during those two days He had stayed at Sychar, He helped her see that He accepted her. When she found acceptance from Him, she realized she could also find forgiveness.

The accounts that Ruth had shared with her, helped her know that He is Love. Here in Jerusalem, she thinks that love was what happened on the cross. It is hard to explain, but all she saw made her say what the soldier said, "Truly, this was the Son of God". Why His Father allowed it to happen, she cannot tell. If someone was killing her son, she would fight back with force. God's restraint, in not destroying those evil men, has shown us His love. She remembers hearing the Man at the well say, "Father, forgive them. They don't realize what they're doing."

Anyway, she had to go. The caravan master said it's time. Delight Days leaves a small gift with Ruth. It's a way of saying thank you. It's a little pot of honey, or as her father called it, amber gold.

Ruth walked two miles with Delight Days, outside Jerusalem. With tears in both of their eyes, they pronounced blessings on one another for Adonai's peace in Christ. They both had their own memories of the man at the well, who He was and is, as well as how their lives had changed because of Him.

Heading Home

The journey home gave Delight Days much time to reflect. On the trip to Jerusalem, there were about forty animals, but now there were at least double that. The caravan would stay on the road to home, then take a route toward the great sea, going up the coast, and then head toward Damascus. The noise and smells from the animals were both deafening and sickening at times. The dust that the animals kicked up was choking. At least this weather had not become sweltering.

Delight Days had time to sort out her emotions. On this, the second day of their trip, she had become aware of two emotions in her heart. So, how can she sum up what has happened to her? Can she find one word that would give clarity to her thoughts?

At first, the word had to be pain, because three crosses gave much pain. Strangely, the pain seemed less now. There was a new hope growing in her soul. She knew that hope was because of the resurrection, yet there had to be a better word that could express her emotions.

As the sun set, and the caravan made camp, no word stuck in her mind. She didn't know why the caravan master was an hour later than usual. Caleb and Delight Days prepared dates, cakes, and cheese with olives for dinner. Following dinner, Delight Days sat at the fire, next to the caravan master.

The night sounds here taking over the animal sounds, as they drifted off to sleep. Softly, the caravan master stated, "Tonight, you will tell me, in your own words, what you saw and if you learned anything."

With guarded breath, Delight Days suddenly became fully aware of her emotions. That one word she had searched for to define her feelings was still evading her.

Sometimes life has moments of clarity. Sitting in the night, by the fire, Delight Days began to tell of the last few days. She shared about her trip to Golgotha, seeing the man from the well, seeing Reuben, learning from Ruth and her understanding about the resurrection. As she spoke, she searched to find meaning in all she had experienced, and to explain what she felt.

The caravan master patiently listened, without interrupting. As the night grew darker, and the stars covered the sky, that word – that one word- had to be said. After all that happened, she told of the new understanding she had. It was about warmth. It is what you feel. Warmth was there on the day of the crucifixion because of Caleb's presence. Ruth, who has become as a sister, gave her warmth. Just being with them brought her warmth. Even the caravan master, by allowing her to go to Jerusalem, provided warmth. You see, she had been alone so long that she never realized her overwhelming need for the warmth of kindness.

For a moment, Delight Days is quiet, hoping her thoughts don't betray her. It is at that moment she realized what her emotions have been screaming out. Quietly, she tells him, "Your warmth and kindness have been a welcoming feeling in my heart." Elder Josiah always said that any time you experience warmth in your life, it is Adonai's grace. He told of Moses wanting to see Adonai's glory. That story is the story of Adonai declaring His grace, by the warmth of His glory. The warmth of what Adonai gives comes from Adonai's character.

One can be in awe of a sunset, and that experience is the warmth of Adonai's grace. Family, friends, fellowship, anytime you are transformed by your experience is Adonai's grace. What she has learned is you must be aware of those times that warm your soul. That is when Adonai's grace is experienced. Her conclusion is she is different because she met the man from the well. She is different because of the resurrection. Her life is different because of His warmth. That warmth of Adonai's grace satisfied Delight Days. Yes, that one word she was looking for was warmth! That feeling in your soul when the heart is overflowing. It is overflowing from what is right and wholesome.

As the fire died, there was no sound. Each one was lost in their own thoughts. Delight Days didn't realize it was getting late as he stood and walked away.

Reflections

Maybe now she can explain her emotions after all that has happened--the preaching of the Gospel by His disciples, the teaching on how the man at the well can bring people into a personal relationship with Adonai.

Delight Days was one of the few who had the opportunity to be at Golgotha that day. She had never tried to explain the significance of that day. It was truly a day of horrors, but now, she can see it more clearly.

First, there was Jehoram, a man who died in his sin. He asked for deliverance, but not forgiveness. For him, it was that he chose not to believe in the Messiah, the man at the well. It seems there are those who are not concerned about life after death.

Second, the other man was Reuben. His belief, that the man from the well was really the Messiah, is what saved him. It is true that initially he rejected the man from the well. It is also true he had become a thief, who was paying for his crimes by the horrible method of crucifixion. But, as they were both dying, Jesus spoke the words only He had the authority to say, "Today, you will join me in Paradise."

Third, the one cross on which she reflects the most, is the middle one. Those who teach His words quote the man at the well saying, "I came to seek and save those who are lost." He lived His life to lay down His life. Reuben and the other thief, well, their lives were taken. Christ's life wasn't taken. It was given! And He gave it to show us how much He loves people!

Yes, that middle cross is where the man at the well ended up. He walked into a city, and a world in desperate need of hope. He came to my city, and my world. There, he had found her, and everyone can be found by Him, just by calling on Him. He found me – a woman with hurts, rejection and a victim of my choices.

He found me and that experience became a wonderful thing in my life. Elder Josiah says, "He is wonderful because He's a wonderful Savior".

Yes, Delight Days can now say she has found true love—even when she had a crisis of faith seven months later. But that's another story.

Epilogue

This story does not end here. In a few months after her return from Jerusalem, Delight Days will experience a crisis of faith. Everyone experiences a moment or even several moments when there is a deep question about one's beliefs.

Delight Days experiences in life are universal in that everyone will sometimes question their faith. Grace seems to be lost in unbelief, doubt or fear and personal wants.

The next book in this series will address Delight Days' crisis of faith.

DEVOTIONALS

This section has three devotional thoughts from the story found in John 4. May they encourage and warm your heart as you examine the woman at the well's story again.

Organic Faith

Today many people talk about organic gardens. The idea is to use nature to rebuild the soil and allow compost to enrich it.

John 4 is unique in that Jesus is trying to build the soil of the soul. The woman at the well needed a new type of faith—that that would and could sustain her. For years the soil of her soul had been depleted by the hardness of life, broken marriages and from being a social outcast.

Faith provides good nutrition for the soul. That is seen in healthy spirituality. Natural compost in the soil becomes natural fertilizer. In the spirit world people are allowing Satan to make the compost. But, when a person uses a Satanic compost to fertilize their soul, they become toxic with doubt, self-hatred, and self-pleasing desires. The spiritual environment and nutritional health becomes depleted.

A Master Gardener like Jesus sees the depleted soul and wants to correct the situation. He does this with the woman at the well—correcting the soil in her soul so that she can have organic faith.

Jesus' reason for going into Samaria was to find a good garden spot. The soil in Judea and Jerusalem had become toxic with religious rejection. Samaria could be a place to build organic faith—natural, alive and healthy for the souls of men.

In meeting the woman at the well, Jesus helped her to consider the relationships of life and faith. The toxic soil of rejection by the Jews and her people as well as her relationships became the environmental destruction of her soul. But Jesus began to work the soil of her soul.

Organic is considered a soil friendly technique used in preparing it for gardening. It is an environmental aid to the soil that does not harm it. In working with her, Jesus was not harsh. Gently He allowed her to experience freedom—the moment when organic faith happens. "Is not this the Christ?" (John 4:29)

"Organic faith will produce a faith that works in life," says Owen. The woman at the well became a fruitful garden of faith, producing in her a willingness to tell all, "Is not this the Christ?"

An Outstanding Day

There are some days that are more memorable than others. For example, the day John F. Kennedy was shot. Some days outshine others—such as your wedding day.

The woman at the well undoubtedly believed that love and marriage would be a great day. But, love can die and it had died for her! It is noon and the sun is very hot and the road is dusty-a day just like many days before. It would be safe to say that this woman had encountered many people in her life. Some good, some bad, some helpful and some not so helpful.

Meeting Jesus will change the woman! That fateful day is not happenstance. It is because God wanted her to meet this man. This meeting with Jesus opened up her understanding to a new truth. You will notice that in John 4:9 she uses the term "Jew". She says to Jesus, "You being a Jew." Was she saying it with disdain? One can only surmise. What is known is that she identified this stranger as a Jew.

As the story unfolds he was moved to use the word, "Sir" (verse 11). "The woman saith unto him, Sir," which is a title of respect. The conversation continues and she says to this Jew, "I perceive that thou art a prophet," which is a foreteller or inspired speaker for God.

From "prophet" she brings up the idea of Messianic hope. She says, "I know that Mesias cometh, which is called Christ: when he is come, he will tell us all things." (Verse 25). She is not yet aware that the Jewish man is the Christ. New truths are being presented and no doubt her mind was working overtime. Jesus had said, "Ye worship ye know not what: we know what we worship: for salvation is of the Jews. " (Verse 22)

Donald Guthrie wrote this about verse 22. "The aim of Jesus was to throw light on the Fatherhood of God." The Jews had more light on this than the Samaritans because salvation was of the Jews—the Messiah was to come from such a source. (Exploring God's Word, page 53)

Jesus' response to this woman is a testimony of a great truth! In verse 26 he says, "I that speak with thee am He". The "He" is the Messiah. Jesus had taken a moment in time and moved this lady to a logical conclusion. Have you ever woke up and said, "Something is different about today." The woman at the well knew it, sensed it, and felt it—Jesus is the Christ! This meeting at the well changed her direction and destiny. Jesus' gift of salvation came from His gift of recognition of her worth and acceptance. And, she sees his worth—Savior! He saw her worth and she became a child of God (John 1:13).

Having found the Christ she became happy, excited and joyful as she went into town and told them, "Come, see this man...is not this the Christ?" (Verse 29).

Go this week and tell someone—"Come see Jesus. Is not this the Christ?" Owen says, "Any day you meet Jesus is an outstanding day."

What is Your Song?

Have you ever felt like saying, "I quit?" Have you ever wanted to just throw up your arms in disgust? Have you ever felt like just walking away from the problem? The woman at the well probably felt that way.

When Jesus told her to "Call your husband" (John 4:16) did that anger her? Was that statement a reminder that her dreams had died a long time ago? Now she is in survival mode. So many use the word "survivor" but some would see defeat.

The show, "Hee Haw", had a sad song that was sung by sad-looking hillbillies. The first line was the apex of defeat—"gloom, despair and agony on me, woe." Defeat is a sad word. It means to be beaten or prevailed over—the complete opposite to winning. Terry Rush says, "Most people believe others can win but not them." That attitude keeps many people from winning.

The Bible is full of people who rose up and defeated their difficulties. The story of the woman at the well is a good example. All of her relationships ended up in smoke—no long term acceptance. In the days of Jesus the idea of a social outcast was deeply ingrained in their thinking. She would know the meaning of gloom, despair and agony. Woe was her song.

The Hee Haw song went on and said, "Deep dark depression, excessive misery." What is excessive misery? It is a life of lacking, of being victimized or having a helpless feeling about your life. It is thinking that life is unfair—being abused or exploited by others or even yourself. Yes, excessive misery is your attitude about how to live life. Owen says, "Only your positive attitude can defeat excessive misery."

The next line in the song says, "If it weren't for bad luck I'd have no luck at all." One easily senses that the Hee Haw song was the song of choice for the woman at the well. But when she met Christ things began to change; Jesus writes her a new song—a song that ends with many in the town saying, "We believe this is the Christ!"

R.E. Hudson wrote about what the woman discovered. "Jesus satisfies my longings, whom my soul so long has craved." It is Jesus who comes, "and heals my broken spirit." (Victory in Jesus)

Don't let the song from "Hee Haw" be your theme song!

Discussion Questions

Reflections on How a Person can Come to a Point Where He Does not See God's Grace

1. Delight Days reflects on all the lack and sadness in life.

   A. Is it possible to see God's grace when you live with lack?

   B. Have you ever felt overwhelmed by lack?

   List three lacks in your life.

   1.

   2.

   3.

   List three loses in your life that affect you.

   1.

   2.

   3.

2. In the chapter "Mid-Morning", pages 21-22, Delight Days explains her feelings. Have you ever felt that way? Write your own paragraph about your own empty feelings and God's grace.

3. In the chapter, "Gone", page 30, Reuben calls God's grace an illusion. Can you relate to that feeling? Explain.

4. What is the best thing for you to do when you feel God's grace is an illusion?

Reflection on the Conversation Between the Woman at the Well and Jesus

(John 4:1-42)

1. You should take the time to read John 4:1-42. Answer these questions.

   A. The woman at the well was thinking in a natural way about water.

      True or False

   B. Jesus was wanting her to think in a spiritual way.

      True or False

C. Jesus is talking about God's gift in John 4:10. What do you think it is?

Look at Romans 1:5 and what it has to say about grace.

D. Did Jesus view this woman with malice, or was it with grace? Why do you think so?

2. Do people today see others with eyes of grace or race? Explain.

3. On page 46, Delight Days felt the disciples were compassionless. Do you think that could happen? Explain.

4. On page 47, Delight Days finds God's grace gives her hope and meaning.

List two things you believe God's grace has given you.

A.

B.

Reflections on the Two Days Jesus Stayed at the City of Sychar

1. The Bible is silent about what Jesus taught during those two days.

List three things you would like to hear Jesus teach if you had two days with Him.

A.

B.

C.

2. On Page 50, Delight Days says, "He did not shun me." Have you ever felt shunned and if so, how did it make you feel?

3. On Page 51, a line says, "always there was a prayer of blessing on each household." What would you think that statement would mean?

4. Pages 55-58 shows a concept about Jesus blessing the children.

Do you pray blessings on your children?

If so, what would your prayer of blessing be?

Reflection on Redemption

1. On page 63, Elder Josiah says that everyone has the opportunity to apply Redemption to their life. For Delight Days it was a new reality. How would you describe your encounter with Jesus?

2. Do you have something like Delight Days had with rocks to help you

remember? What is it?

3. On page72, Reuben feels that the people who listen to God or the man at the well are simpletons. What does this mean to you?

4. Reuben states that money was his grace on page 73. Do people trust in money more than God in America today?

Reflection About the Road to Jerusalem

1. On pages 76-77, Delight Days reflects on where is "here". She tries to explain what "here" means to her. Can we say that "here" is moments of experiencing God's grace? What are some times you have experienced God's grace?

2. On page 94, Reuben says, "I'm sorry. I want you to know I have found God's grace". During your life, have you seen God's Grace become an overwhelming awareness of God's love? Explain.

3. On Page 102, Delight Days gives Ruth a little pot of honey. Can you say that your acts of kindness are really acts of grace to others?

List three things you feel could be acts of grace.

A.

B.

C.

Reflection on the Crosses: Finding the True Meaning of Grace

1. On page 103-106, Delight Days tries to express her emotions and to explain what she feels. If you would have been at the cross, what do you think you would have felt? Write three sentences about your emotions.

2. Read Exodus 34:6-7. God make a personal confession about His nature.

Can you say this passage shows God as full of grace? Explain.

3. Pages 107-108 gives us Delight Days' reflections of the three crosses and the impact on her life. In your own words, write about the impact in your life for each of the crosses.

    A. The thief who rejected Christ

    B. The thief who received Christ

    C. Christ

www.ingramcontent.com/pod-product-compliance
Lightning Source LLC
Chambersburg PA
CBHW071821020426
42331CB00007B/1574